LIVING
THE GOOD LIFE
TOGETHER

ATTENTIVENESS
being present

study & reflection guide

Susan Pendleton Jones
and L. Gregory Jones

ABINGDON PRESS / Nashville

LIVING THE GOOD LIFE TOGETHER
ATTENTIVENESS: BEING PRESENT
Study & Reflection Guide

Copyright © 2006 by Abingdon Press

This book is printed on acid-free, elemental chlorine-free paper.

ISBN 0-687-46540-0

06 07 08 09 10 11 12 13 14 15—10 9 8 7 6 5 4 3 2 1
MANUFACTURED IN THE UNITED STATES OF AMERICA

Contents

—1—

An Introduction to This Study Series

PSALM FOR PRAYING

Psalm 84:1-4

How lovely is your dwelling place,
  O LORD of hosts!
My soul longs, indeed it faints
  for the courts of the LORD;
my heart and my flesh sing for joy
  to the living God.

Even the sparrow finds a home,
  and the swallow a nest for herself,
  where she may lay her young,
at your altars, O LORD of hosts,
  my King and my God.
Happy are those who live in your house,
  ever singing your praise.

CHRISTIAN CHARACTER IN COMMUNITY

THE GREAT EARLY Christian theologian Augustine opens his *Confessions* with these famous words: "Restless is our heart until it comes to rest in thee." Augustine, who had himself led a life of distorted and disordered desires that left him frustrated and without satisfaction, eventually discovered that we only find satisfaction when we rest in God. We are created for life with God, and only through God's love will we discover the rest, wholeness, and fullness we most truly desire.

So how can we discover this fullness of life that we yearn for, especially when we try and try but can't seem to get any satisfaction? Ironically, we will only discover it when we quit trying so hard. Instead, we need to learn to rest in God, the God who loves us and embraces us before we can do anything. God's grace invites us to discover that we cannot earn love; we can only discover it in the gift of being loved.

So far, so good. But it seems easier said than done. After all, to receive the gift of being loved calls for us to love in return. And yet we lack the skills—and often the desire—to love in the way God loves us. As a result, as wonderful as it sounds to "rest in God," to discover "the gift of being loved by God," we fear that we are not up to the relationship.

In order to truly receive love, we want to become like the lover. So for us to truly receive God's love, we are called to become like God—and that sounds both inviting and scary. Become like God? This becomes even more daunting when we discover that this gracious, loving God is also the one who is called "holy" and calls us through God's love to be holy as well. Jesus even enjoins us to be "perfect" as our "heavenly Father is perfect" (Matthew 5:48). The task begins to seem overwhelming. How does this relate to the idea of resting in God's grace?

The wonder and joy of Christian life is that we are invited by God into a way of life, a life of abundance in which we learn to cultivate habits of desiring, thinking, feeling, and living that continually open us to the grace of God's holiness. The invitation to Christian life is an invitation to discover that "the good life" is lived in the light of God's grace. When we embark on a truly Christian life, we learn to become holy not by trying really hard but by continually being drawn into the disciplined habits of living as friends of God in the community of others.

This may seem odd at first, but think about it in terms of learning to play the piano. We're drawn by the desire to play beautiful music. But before we can play beautiful music, we have to learn basic habits: the position of our hands, the scales of the piano, the role of the foot pedals, and the rhythms of music. Over time, as we learn these basic skills, our teachers invite us to take on more challenging tasks. Eventually, we find ourselves playing with both hands, learning to master more complicated arrangements of music, and perhaps even integrating the foot pedals into our playing. If we practice the piano long enough, we will reach a point where it seems effortless to play—and even to improvise new music—in the company of others.

It's around this metaphor of practice that Living the Good Life Together: A Study of Christian Character in Community has been developed. Rather than to practice being piano players, this series of small-group studies is aimed at helping persons practice being Christian. Each unit of study is designed to move persons from *understanding* various aspects of Christian character to the development of *practices* reflective of those aspects of Christian character to, ultimately, the *embodiment* of Christian character in community. In other words, the idea is to educate the desires of heart and mind in order to develop, over time, patterns of living like Christ.

A billboard or bumper sticker would say it more succinctly: "The Good Life: Get It. Try It. Live It—Together."

Living the Good Life Together gets at the heart of the life God intends for us, particularly as it relates to others in community. Attentiveness, forgiveness, discernment, intimacy, humility, hospitality—these are some of the aspects of the life God intends for us. And they are the subjects of this study series.

STUDY FORMAT

The overall process of this study series is based on some of Jesus' own words to his followers: "Come and see" (John 1:39) and "Go and do likewise" (Luke 10:37). In each study, the first six sessions are the backbone of the "Come and See" portion. These sessions inspire and teach the group about a particular character trait of the Christian life. The second six sessions are the "Go and Do" portion. For these sessions, the study offers tools to help group members plan how to put into practice what they have learned.

"Come and See"

Session 1: An Introduction to This Study Series

This session is an orientation to the twelve-week study. It provides information about the Living the Good Life Together series and an introduction to the trait of Christian character addressed in that particular study.

Sessions 2–5: Topics in Christian Character

These sessions offer information about aspects of the particular trait of Christian character. The sessions will help group members explore the trait and will foster intimacy with Scripture, with others, and with God.

Session 6: Planning the Next Steps Together

In this session, group members plan what they will do together in Sessions 7–12 to practice the Christian character trait they have learned about in the previous sessions.

"Go and Do"

Sessions 7–12: From Study to Practice

In these sessions, group members will carry out their plans from Session 6, putting their learnings into practice.

USING THE RESOURCE COMPONENTS

The resource components of Living the Good Life Together—the study & reflection guide, leader guide, and DVD—and the group sessions function together to foster intimacy with Scripture, with others, and with God. This takes place through a broad range of approaches: reading, writing, discussion, viewing video, prayer, worship, and practical application.

Study & Reflection Guide

This book serves as a guide for individual preparation from week to week, as a personal journal for responding to all elements of the study, and as a planning tool for the "Go and Do" portion of the study. Becoming familiar with the following content sections will enhance the effectiveness of this guide.

Psalm for Praying

A psalm text appears on the first page of each session of the study & reflection guide. It's there for you to use as a prayer of invocation as you begin your study each day.

Daily Readings

Reading these passages each day is central to your preparation for the group meeting. Consider reading from different translations of the Bible to hear familiar texts in a fresh way. Ask what the Scriptures mean in light of the session's theme and how they apply to your own life. Be alert to insights and questions you would like to remember for the group meeting, and jot those down in the boxes provided in this study & reflection guide.

Reflections

The space at the bottom of each page in each content session of the study & reflection guide is provided for making notes or recording any thoughts or questions the reading brings to mind.

Lectio Divina

Each session of this study will include a prayer exercise called *lectio divina*, sometimes called "praying the Scriptures." The practice of lectio divina, which is Latin for "sacred reading," continues to gain popularity as people discover anew this ancient and meaningful approach to prayer.

In the practice of lectio divina outlined below, we listen, as the Benedictines instruct, "with the ear of the heart" for a word, phrase, sound, or image that holds a special meaning for us. This could be a word of comfort, instruction, challenge, or assurance. It could be an image suggested by a word, and the image could take us to a place of deep reverence or personal introspection.

It's important to note that like the biblical exercises in this book, lectio divina is about what is evoked in you as you experience the text. Now is not the time for historical-critical musings or scholarly interpretations of the text. It's time for falling in love with the Word and experiencing the goodness of God.

Step One: *Silencio.* After everyone has turned to the Scripture, be still. Silently turn all your thoughts and desires over to God. Let go of concerns, worries, or agendas. Just *be* for a few minutes.

Step Two: *Lectio.* Read the short passage of Scripture slowly and carefully, either aloud or silently. Reread it. Be alert to any word, phase, or image that invites you, that puzzles you, that intrigues you. Wait for this word, phrase, or image to come to you; try not to rush it.

Step Three: *Meditatio.* Take the word, phrase, or image from your Scripture passage that comes to you and ruminate over it. Repeat it to yourself. Allow this word, phrase, or image to engage your thoughts, your desires, your memories. You may share your word, phrase, or image with others in the group, but don't feel pressured to speak.

Step Four: *Oratio.* Pray that God transform you through the word, phrase, or image from Scripture. Consider how this word, phrase, or image connects with your life and how God is made known to you in it. This prayer may be either silent or spoken.

Step Five: *Contemplatio.* Rest silently in the presence of God. Move beyond words, phrases, or images. Again, just *be* for a few minutes. Close this time of lectio divina with "Amen."[1]

Faithful Friends

True friends in faith are those who can help us hear the voice of God in our lives more clearly. They act as our mentors, our guides. At times they weep with us, and at other times they laugh with us. At all times they keep watch over us in love and receive our watch-care in return. Having a faithful friend (or friends) and being a faithful friend are at the heart of what it means to live as a Christian in community for at least three reasons:

- Faithful friends can at times challenge the sins we have come to love.
- Faithful friends will affirm the gifts we are afraid to claim.
- Faithful friends help us dream the dreams we otherwise wouldn't have imagined.

During this study, each group member will be invited to join with one or two others to practice being a faithful friend over the course of the twelve weeks and hopefully beyond. While there are no "mystical" qualifications for being a faithful friend, what *is* required is the willingness to be open to possibilities of guiding another person or persons into a deeper and richer experience of Christian living. Like all aspects of the Christian life, this activity of being a faithful friend is a discipline, a practice.

A key decision faithful friends will make is how to stay in touch week after week. Some may choose to meet over lunch or coffee or take a walk. Others may choose to use e-mail or the telephone. Whatever the means, consider using the following questions to stimulate an ongoing conversation over the course of the study:

- How has it gone for you, trying to live the week's practice?
- What's been hard about it?
- What's been easy or comfortable?
- What challenges have there been? What rewards?
- What kinds of things happened this week—at work, at home, in your prayer life—that you want to talk about? Has anything affected your spiritual life and walk?

There's an old African proverb that says, "If you want to go fast, go alone. If you want to go far, go together." In the end, a faithful friend is someone who is willing to go the distance with you, following Christ all the way. The aim of this feature of the study is to move you further down the way of Christian discipleship in the company of another.

ATTENTIVENESS: BEING PRESENT

We've been introduced to the study series Living the Good Life Together. Now it's time to turn our attention to the particular trait of Christian character that we'll be exploring and focusing upon throughout this study: *attentiveness.*

Attentiveness is a basic skill in all human life. As children, we were taught to pay attention so that we might learn. We were taught to stop, look, and listen so that we might be safe. Human activities such as driving, operating machinery or computers, farming and gardening, cooking, playing a musical instrument, caring for children, entertaining guests, reading a book, going to a play, or watching a movie require attentiveness. In fact, it's challenging to think of a human activity other than sleep that does not in some way involve attentiveness.

Since attentiveness is such a basic practice in daily human existence, we may at first wonder why it is considered an important trait of Christian character. Exploring the meanings of the word *attentiveness* offers insight. To attend is to be present, to take care of or look after, to listen to or look at. The word comes from ancient roots that mean to stretch toward something. All these shimmers of meaning radiate from attentiveness. *Christian attentiveness* is the practice of being present, looking, listening, stretching toward God and toward God's ways of life revealed in the world, in Scripture, and through Jesus Christ.

The meanings of the word *attentiveness* contain as a key component an active response of caring for or looking after something or someone. Be still, stop, look, and listen to God; then act according to God's ways. Jesus said, "Come and see" (John 1:39), then "Go and do likewise"(Luke 10:37). Be both hearers and doers of the word (Matthew 7:24; James 1:22-25). "Attending to" the Christian character trait of attentiveness to God opens our minds and hearts to God's grace, power, and steadfast love. As we practice attentiveness, we discover God's transforming life. The Scripture says this yet another way: "Seek, and you will find" (Matthew 7:7, NKJV). If we seek God and God's ways through the practice of attentiveness, we will find what we need to live God's way.

Jesus encouraged attentiveness when he spoke about eyes that see (Mark 8:18; Luke 10:23) and ears that hear (Mark 4:9, 23; Luke 8:8; 14:35). The next five sessions in ATTENTIVENESS: BEING PRESENT rely upon the idea of listening in order to teach about and put into practice several aspects of attentiveness. Session 2, "Listening to the Right Voices," deals with listening to the voice of God in our noisy world. Session 3, "Keeping Time," encourages us to make time to listen to God. Session 4, "Self-Awareness," challenges us to see ourselves as God sees us. Session 5, "Listening Alone, Listening Together," invites us to pray alone and to pray with others. Session 6, "Planning the Next Steps Together," facilitates the group planning process for putting into practice what members have learned about attentiveness. All the sessions help us to "stretch toward" God and practice God's ways of attentiveness.

Pay attention. Stop. Look. Listen. Be still. Be present to God. Come and see the practice of attentiveness. Then go and do likewise.

—2—

Listening to the Right Voices

Psalm 42:1-6a

As a deer longs for flowing
    streams,
  so my soul longs for you,
    O God.
My soul thirsts for God,
  for the living God.
When shall I come and behold
  the face of God?
My tears have been my food
  day and night,
while people say to me
    continually,
  "Where is your God?"

These things I remember,
  as I pour out my soul:
how I went with the throng,
  and led them in procession
    to the house of God,
with glad shouts and songs of
    thanksgiving,
  a multitude keeping festival.
Why are you cast down,
    O my soul,
  and why are you disquieted
    within me?
Hope in God; for I shall again
    praise him,
  my help and my God.

DAILY READINGS

DAY ONE
1 Kings 19:11-15 *(The sound of God is sheer silence)*

DAY TWO
Matthew 6:25-34 *(The lilies of the field)*

DAY THREE
Acts 15:1, 22-29 *(Discerning among different teachings)*

DAY FOUR
Romans 12:1-2 *(Be transformed, not conformed)*

DAY FIVE
1 John 4:13-16 *(God is love; those who abide in love abide in God)*

DAY SIX
Read the chapter on pages 20–25. You may take notes in the space provided at the bottom of each page.

CHRISTIANS ARE CALLED "people of the Word." Whether the Word is Scripture printed on the pages of our well-worn Bibles or the words we hear proclaimed Sunday after Sunday from the pulpits of our churches, in order to understand the Word—to take it in properly, to digest it well—we have to learn to be good listeners. It means we have to focus, to unclutter our minds from anxieties and distractions, and to pay attention to what we read and hear. Scripture calls us to move beyond ourselves, to imagine life outside the confines of our narrow frames of reference, to hear God speaking in a way that changes how we think and how we live. In our fast-paced, filled-to-capacity consumer culture, it's not easy for God to get our attention. And this is even more reason for us to focus intentionally on learning how to become good listeners, learning to be attentive—attentive, that is, to the right voices.

CHRISTIAN CHARACTER IN CONTEXT

The Bible uses the Hebrew word *hinneh* nearly a thousand times. We usually translate it as "behold," but it can also mean "Hey, check it out!" "Listen up!" or "Wow!"[2] Hinneh is an attention-grabbing word. Angels say it, prophets say it, and even Jesus says a form of it when he wants to get people's attention. This word reminds us that God has something important to say to us and wants to get our attention. It means we have to unclutter our lives enough to be able to listen.

When our oldest son was three years old, he loved to watch cartoons, not so much for the cartoons but for the commercials between the cartoons. He saw some cool action figures, kids on

reflections

shiny new bikes, and tempting new breakfast cereals. He thought this was the greatest stuff. He would come to us after watching those commercials and say, "I need this. I want that. Buy this for me." Each day he would add more things to the list. Finally, we sat down with him and we said, "Nathan, they're trying to trick you." He looked up at us at age three and said, "But I want to be tricked. I really like this stuff. I want to be tricked."

People have never had more choices than we do today. Try to buy a pair of jeans, and you're confronted with a host of options: slim fit, easy fit, relaxed fit, baggy fit, regular or faded, stone washed, acid washed, straight leg, flair leg, or no leg. A friend of ours bought a house that had a microwave built into it. The microwave had so many buttons and bells and whistles she decided to use it simply as a breadbox. One time we started to warm up some food in it, and she said, "No, no, no, the bread and the rolls are stored in there."

Barry Schwartz, Professor of Social Theory and Social Action at Swarthmore College, has written a book called *The Paradox of Choice: Why More Is Less.* We have so much more to choose from than any other generation, and at first glance this may look like a great thing. But the rate of clinical depression in the U.S. has increased dramatically in the last twenty-five years. Ironically, more choice often means less happiness. And yet, the world always tries to convince us that more is always better. So, in the midst of all these choices, all the noises in our lives, all these competing voices, how do we respond faithfully without being distracted—or worse, "co-opted"—by the choices? Who are we going to allow to

Ironically, more choice often means less happiness.

reflections

21

shape our lives? Somebody's going to do it. Is it our friends? Our spouse? Wall Street, Madison Avenue, and our consumer culture? Is it ourselves? Is it God? When there are so many competing voices and so many different choices in our lives, how do we hear the voice of God in the midst of all the options? How do we know when we're listening well?

TO BE CONFORMED OR NOT TO BE

In Romans 12:2, Paul says, "Do not be conformed to this world, but be transformed by the renewing of your minds, so that you may discern what is the will of God—what is good and acceptable and perfect." The "world" that Paul speaks of is not a geographical place but a mentality, a driving influence that says you are the most important thing that exists. Turn on the television or pick up a newspaper, and advertisements will remind you that we live in a "what's in it for me" society. We live in a world of disordered desire where we are paralyzed by too many choices, where all the pressures are on us to join the crowd, to conform, to put ourselves and our needs first. This is not the world of God's good creation; it is the world marked by sin, greed, and often violence and destruction.

James 3:16 describes this world in terms of "envy and selfish ambition." It is the world we are *born* into, but it is very different from the one we are *baptized* into. These two worlds compete for our allegiance. The world we are born into is the one we are surrounded by most of the time, and often we don't even realize its influence on our lives because we are so used to it.

How do we see beyond the world of "envy and selfish ambition" and begin to understand the world we are baptized into? How do

reflections

we discern the Spirit with a capital "S" from all the spirits that are alive in the world? And those other spirits are out there. There's a good reason that when we talk about alcohol, we use the word *spirits* because alcohol so often leads us down irrational paths. Sports teams can sometimes create a kind of mob scene of "spirit" that doesn't draw people together but rather divides them. We are too often influenced by the "spirit" of this designer or that entertainer. All sorts of spirits are alive out in the world.

TESTING THE SPIRITS

How do we test the spirits to discern which ones are consistent with God's Spirit and which ones are destructive? There is a remarkable story in Acts 15 about the Council of Jerusalem. In this passage, followers of Jesus are trying to answer the question, "How is Jesus supposed to shape my life?" Those gathered hold different opinions on the subject of whether Gentiles need to become Jewish in order to follow Jesus—or more specifically, whether males need to be circumcised in order to follow Jesus. So a number of "apostles and...elders" (15:6) meet in Jerusalem to determine what God is calling them to do.

What is significant about the Council of Jerusalem is the conclusion that they reach. Toward the end of Acts 15, at the close of the council's deliberations, we read, "It has seemed good to the Holy Spirit and to us..." (v. 28). What is missing from that formulation is the pronoun *me*. The text doesn't say, "It has seemed good to me, and I hope the Spirit and the rest of you are willing to go along," or "It has seemed good to me," period. The council's focus is on the Spirit and on what is best for all. Clearly these early church leaders were attentive to the workings of the Holy Spirit.

reflections

LISTENING FOR THE VOICE OF GOD AND LISTENING TO THE VOICES OF OTHERS

Focusing on the Spirit and what is best for others will provide a big challenge to the "what's in it for me" mentality that shapes so much of our lives. By implication, we Christians today must learn how to listen for the voice of God and be attentive to the voices of others around us. Of course, we occasionally listen to God in prayer, and we occasionally listen to God by reading and studying Scripture. But studying Scripture has to be done consistently in a listening mode. Too much of the time, when we turn to Scripture, we are looking for ways to justify positions we already hold. We are looking for ammunition for an argument or to score points. By contrast, it is very different actually to listen for God's voice, to listen and attend to what God might be saying to us—sometimes in spite of us—as we hear to what is being said. Often we discover that in reading Scripture, Scripture is actually reading us. If we read it carefully and with an open mind, Scripture challenges our assumptions and calls us to live in a way we otherwise might not choose.

Often we discover that in reading Scripture, Scripture is actually reading us.

To be attentive to the voices of others around us, we must listen to them, for by listening to how different people hear God speak, we discover how their wisdom and experience can guide and shape our own lives. One of the greatest challenges in listening to others is putting aside our own thoughts, issues, and arguments. We have

reflections

a friend who is never able to hear someone tell a story without having to immediately share a similar story about his life. He isn't really listening to what the other person is saying; he's hearing the other person only as that person's experience reflects on his own. All of us do this to a certain degree, but when we are unable to see this tendency, then we become blind to the ways in which we fail to listen.

There was a group of people at a college who were having difficulty getting along with each other. They hired a consultant to help them communicate. After meeting with them and watching them interact, her recommendation was that in future meetings, before anyone could speak, the current speaker had to summarize the statement made by the previous speaker to that person's satisfaction before making his or her own statement. This practice requires that first you must learn how to become a good listener—and only then can you can become a good conversation partner.

The words carved on the front of the Communion table in our school chapel are "I THIRST." These two words echo not only Jesus' words from the cross but also the psalmist's longing for God in Psalm 42:1-2: "My soul longs for you, O God. / My soul thirsts for God." As we draw upon this longing, this desire to know God, we will discover that listening more attentively to the voice of God—and to the voices of others who journey with us in faith—is one of the greatest gifts we can receive in living the good life together.

reflections

FAITHFUL FRIENDS: WATCHING OVER ONE ANOTHER IN LOVE

Use this space to record thoughts, reflections, insights, prayer concerns, or other matters that arise from your weekly conversations with faithful friends.

—3—

Keeping Time

Psalm 90:1-2; 14-17

Lord, you have been our
dwelling place
in all generations.
Before the mountains were
brought forth,
or ever you had formed the
earth and the world,
from everlasting to
everlasting you are God.
....
Satisfy us in the morning with
your steadfast love,
so that we may rejoice and be
glad all our days.

Make us glad as many days as
you have afflicted us,
and as many years as we have
seen evil.
Let your work be manifest to
your servants,
and your glorious power to
their children.
Let the favor of the Lord our
God be upon us,
and prosper for us the work
of our hands—
O prosper the work of our
hands!

DAILY READINGS

DAY ONE
Genesis 1:1-5 *(The creation of evening and morning)*

DAY TWO
Exodus 20:1-17; Deuteronomy 5:1-21 *(The Ten Commandments)*

DAY THREE
Mark 2:23–3:6 *(The sabbath was made for humankind)*

DAY FOUR
John 1:1-18 *(The Word became flesh)*

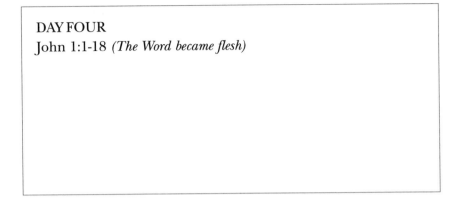

DAY FIVE
Galatians 4:4-7 *(No longer a slave but a child and an heir)*;
Galatians 5:16-23 *(The fruit of the Spirit)*

DAY SIX
*Read the chapter on pages 30–35. You may take notes in the space
provided at the bottom of each page.*

OUR LIVES ARE NOT only overflowing with "things" but also tend to be filled to capacity with demands and time constraints. It's called "calendar clutter." Computer calendars are even programmed to allow us to book ourselves to be in several different places at once. For most of us, it seems there just aren't enough hours in the day to get everything done. Work concerns, family concerns, church concerns, civic concerns.... We can accomplish more because things have never happened as fast as they do in the twenty-first century. A push of a button can mean an electronic message sent to a friend on another continent within a matter of seconds or a hassle-free means of banking. We want it done now; ideally, we want it done yesterday. Because we can accomplish so much so quickly, it naturally follows that we expect to get more done. So the issue becomes a question of focus. How do we choose between what seems urgent and what really is important? How do we focus on the important without being distracted by all the other less important possibilities?

CHRISTIAN CHARACTER IN OUR LIVES

One of our favorite Bible stories is Jesus' visit to Mary and Martha. Luke 10:38-42 tells us that Martha is "distracted" by her many tasks of preparing the meal. When she notices that Mary is sitting and listening to what Jesus has to say, she comes into the room and asks Jesus if he cares that her sister has left her to do all the work by herself. "Tell her then to help me," she says. Jesus surprises her with his answer. "Martha, Martha, you are worried and distracted by many things; there is need of only one thing. Mary has chosen the better part, which will not be taken away from her."

reflections

_____

_____

_____

_____

_____

What Martha was doing had a certain temporal importance, but what Mary was doing was the one necessary thing that would last a lifetime. Martha needed to move away from being distracted by the many things and change her priorities to reflect the one necessary thing, which Mary's sitting and listening to Jesus represents.

To move from the "many things" to the "one thing" was the challenge for Martha, who lived in first-century Palestine. Imagine how much more difficult it is for those of us who live in twenty-first-century North America to do the same. We have far more choices and complexities in our lives—far more distractions—because of the abundance of opportunities and demands that our modern, high-tech, consumer culture offers. But we are called, like Martha, to relocate the center of our attention—to live without allowing these distractions to become the main focus of our lives. We need to have God firmly rooted at the center of everything. Yet, if we are honest with ourselves, we will admit that we are constantly surrounded by distractions.

Only when we establish a new rhythm to our lives will we be able to shift the focus of our attention. This rhythm is countercultural to the 24/7 world we inhabit. It involves learning to wait (the seasons of Advent and Lent help us in this), deferring gratification, taking the focus off productivity, and cultivating *patience*—one of the nine fruits of the Spirit that Paul writes about in Galatians 5. If we look in Exodus 20, the rhythm that Scripture suggests—actually, commands—is called *sabbath-keeping*. This commandment is located just after the first three (20:2-7), which focus on our relationship with God, and just before the last six (20:12-17), which focus on our relationship with others. The sabbath commandment is the "bridge" that links our relationship with God to our relationship with others. The command to rest

reflections

relates to the human need to slow down so that we might be attentive to God as well as be attentive to how we relate to others.

This rhythm of sabbath-keeping was established from the very beginning of time. We first hear about it in Genesis. When God finishes the work of creation, God looks back over the work of those six days—over each one of those days—and realizes that it isn't just good, it's "very good" (Genesis 1:31). Instead of continuing on—fine-tuning, perfecting, fiddling with the handiwork of creation to try to make it very, very, very good—God stops. God takes a day off to take pleasure in all that has been created, to delight in this very good world.

GOD'S EXAMPLE

To follow God's example, we too need to know when to stop, when things are good enough, when we've done all we can do. Even God stopped to say, "What I've done is very good. I should rest now." As Dorothy Bass puts it in *Receiving the Day*, we have to step off the "treadmill of working and spending on which we scurry."[3] The sabbath reminds us that we are not ultimately in control. Human effort doesn't supply the rain and the sunshine, the day and the night that bring about the harvest.

The sabbath reminds us that we are not ultimately in control.

Sabbath rest is not something we earn by staying busy enough or productive enough during the rest of the week. When you carefully read the Creation story at the end of Genesis 1, you see that because Adam and Eve are created on the sixth day, the first thing

reflections

they experience is sabbath. Before they could have earned it or before it could be understood as the reward for a good week's work, they are offered the sabbath day. So the sabbath must be received as a gift as well as a command.

But there is another important purpose for the sabbath, and that is worship. Genesis 2:3 tells us that God "blessed the seventh day and hallowed it." God names it holy. And because we have been created in the image of God, we too are to observe the sabbath as a holy day, set apart from all others.

While God's example of sabbath-keeping is found in Genesis, the sabbath commandment is found in both Exodus 20:8-11 and in Deuteronomy 5:12-15. And in addition to being a significant element in the Creation story, this concept of sabbath is conspicuous in two other important biblical stories: the Exodus and the Resurrection.

In Exodus 20, the focus of sabbath-keeping is on its context in *Creation*. God blesses the sabbath day by resting on it to hallow it. And since we have been created in God's image, we are called to remember the sabbath, to follow the pattern God set of resting.

In Deuteronomy 5, the people are called to observe the sabbath in gratitude for the *Exodus*, literally, their "road out" or liberation from bondage in Egypt. "Remember that you were a slave in the land of Egypt, and the LORD your God brought you out from there with a mighty hand" (v. 15). For six days they are to work; on the seventh they are commanded to rest. Slaves would normally not be granted a day off, but here they are given this day of rest. Here then, sabbath rest is set in the context of liberation—freedom from enforced servitude, which makes the day of rest a social justice concern.

reflections

The sabbath is also linked in Scripture to the *Resurrection*. Each sabbath day—traditionally every Sunday for Christians—is a little Easter, a celebration of the Resurrection and new life that we find in Christ. On the sabbath, we celebrate Christ's victory over the powers of sin and death and experience anew the gift of forgiveness and grace freely offered to us by God.

JESUS AND THE SABBATH

Jesus challenges the rigid interpretation of the sabbath by the religious leaders of his day. He allows his disciples to pluck grain on the sabbath. He heals on the sabbath and then states clearly, "The sabbath was made for humankind, and not humankind for the sabbath" (Mark 2:27). Jesus regularly put people and their needs above principles or rigid interpretations of the law. His understanding of sabbath helps us see it as *prescriptive* rather than *proscriptive*—that is, it is a day to focus on good, useful things that are edifying to ourselves and others rather than a day of prohibitions.

Jesus regularly put people and their needs above principles or rigid interpretations of the law.

However, Jesus does limit the amount of work his disciples are allowed to do in general. After Jesus had sent the disciples out two by two and empowered them with his authority, they return to him and they tell him all they have done and taught. Rather than telling them to go out and do more, he responds by saying, "Come away to a deserted place all by yourselves and rest a while" (Mark 6:31). Jesus was reminding them that in order to be attentive to the voice of

reflections

God, they needed time apart, and by doing so, he reminded them that they were not the ones in control. God's work could continue on even if they took time away for proper rest.

How we view time is central to paying attention to God and listening for God's voice. We can understand time as *chronos,* which is linear time that moves minute by minute, hour by hour into the future. We mark it by the ticking of the clock, ripping pages from the calendar, and marking off anniversaries. We try to minimize its effects by using "anti-aging" creams, getting rid of the gray, or participating in a heightened exercise program. But there is another form of time that we might call "in-breaking" time. In the New Testament, the word *kairos* is used to describe a fulfilled time (Mark 1:15), an opportune time (Galatians 6:9), time beyond time. A friend once described a sermon she heard as a kairos moment. It is time that grabs our attention and holds on to it—and takes us out of ourselves and lifts us upward toward God.

But the opposite is true as well. When God comes down to us and dwells in our midst, it's also kairos time. We call it *incarnation*— God's coming in human form as the Word made flesh. We believe that this same Word who was with God in Creation, at the beginning of all time, came to live among us in the one called Christ and will come again in glory at the end of time. This one who is the same "yesterday and today and forever" (Hebrews 13:8) has come to live among us so that we might truly come to know God. When we are most attentive to God's presence in our midst, then we truly begin to live the good life.

reflections

FAITHFUL FRIENDS: WATCHING OVER ONE ANOTHER IN LOVE

Use this space to record thoughts, reflections, insights, prayer concerns, or other matters that arise from your weekly conversations with faithful friends.

Self-Awareness

PSALM FOR PRAYING

Psalm 139:1-3, 23-24

O LORD, you have searched me
    and known me.
You know when I sit down and
    when I rise up;
    you discern my thoughts
    from far away.
You search out my path and my
    lying down,
    and are acquainted with all
    my ways.

....

Search me, O God, and know
    my heart;
    test me and know my
    thoughts.
See if there is any wicked way
    in me,
    and lead me in the way
    everlasting.

DAILY READINGS

DAY ONE
Isaiah 35 *(The ransomed of the Lord return to Zion)*

DAY TWO
Matthew 17:1-8 *(The Transfiguration)*;
Matthew 5:1-11 *(The Sermon on the Mount)*

DAY THREE
Mark 7:24-30 *(The Gentile woman intercedes for her daughter)*

DAY FOUR

Romans 7:15-25a *(The Law is spiritual, but we struggle with the flesh)*

DAY FIVE

James 2:14-26 *(What good is it if you have faith but not works?)*

DAY SIX

Read the chapter on pages 40–45. You may take notes in the space provided at the bottom of each page.

THERE WAS A FAMILY WHO drove through Kentucky on their way to Toronto, Canada. They did a little sightseeing along the way and stopped at Sloan's Pond, a creek known in the backwoods of Kentucky for its huge bullfrogs. The four of them got out of the car, went down a makeshift pier, and sat at the edge of the pond and waited. After a few quiet moments, one frog appeared, then two, then three, four, five—soon dozens of frogs were croaking in harmony. As the family sat there listening to the beautiful sounds of nature, another car pulled up, and two people got out. Hearing the sound of the car, the frogs in the pond quickly disappeared. Hurriedly and noisily the two tourists came to the edge of the pond, hoping to hear and see the frogs. Soon one of them said, "I guess the word we heard about great frogs at Sloan's Pond was just an overblown story. There don't seem to be any frogs here anymore." And after a few more minutes of talking, pacing the pier, and making more than their share of noise, they got back in their car and left, sure that there were no longer frogs to be found at Sloan's Pond.

The other family stayed where they were for a few more minutes, and sure enough, once it was quiet, the frogs reappeared one by one and began serenading the family again. As the family returned to their car and continued on their journey toward Canada, they reflected on what it must be like to go through life like those two tourists—too busy to be able to see the wonders of the world around them, so noisy and preoccupied with themselves that they were unable to experience what they had driven all that way to hear. And they were likely to tell others that there are no more frogs at Sloan's Pond.

reflections

CHRISTIAN CHARACTER IN CONTEXT

Jesus spoke a lot about how we see and how we hear: "Let anyone with ears to hear listen!" (Mark 4:9). Some people, no matter how well their ears work, never really hear. Other people, no matter how well their eyes work, never really see. They neither hear nor see the mysteries of God revealed around them. Perhaps they are too busy, or maybe they are self-deceived, or perhaps they don't have the imagination to see God at work in ways they might not expect.

We are challenged in Scripture to see God in very unlikely places: in the face of the poor, in an outcast Gentile woman, and in a young girl possessed by a demon. James 2:5 says, "Has not God chosen the poor in the world to be rich in faith and to be heirs of the kingdom?" We need to be attentive to God at work not only in the places that we would expect but also, as Rowan Williams puts it, in the connections that we cannot make.[4]

Too often the church has looked for God in places where the world tells us God should be. The church has frequently sided with the rich, the powerful, and the countries that have military might. In his book *The Culture of Disbelief,* Stephen Carter reminds us how over the centuries the church has

> **Too often the church has looked for God in places where the world tells us God should be.**

failed to see God and has allowed itself to become an instrument of evil. During the Middle Ages, the church would castrate little boys to improve their voices for church choirs. During the Inquisition, thousands were killed in God's name. Even during

reflections

41

the Nazi regime of the last century, the established church by and large sided with Hitler, offering little voice and stifled opposition to the killing of millions of Jews and other minority groups.[5] We should not think that just because we are the church, we always have "eyes...to see" and "ears...to hear" (Mark 8:18).

It's not only the church that needs to confess and admit wrongdoing. As individual Christians, we need to confess our busyness (often masquerading as a sign of how truly important we think we are) and our preoccupation with our own concerns (our consumer society tends to drive us in this direction). But we must also pray to overcome something much more difficult to see and to acknowledge: our own self-deception. This is why we need to pray with the psalmist, "Search me, O God, and know my heart; / test me and know my thoughts. / See if there is any wicked way in me, / and lead me in the way everlasting" (Psalm 139:23-24). We must examine our own hearts as well as develop trusting relationships with others who are wise and who know us well so that they may help lead us to the truth. Coming to see and admit our faults or shortcomings is not intended to lead to self-renunciation but rather to move us toward the freedom and joy of God's fresh forgiveness. Only when we come to know *whose* we are do we fully know *who* we are.

WHO AM I?

When German theologian and pastor Dietrich Bonhoeffer was imprisoned by the Nazis during World War II, he wrote this poem seeking God's guidance in understanding the limitations of his own self-awareness.

reflections

Who am I? They often tell me
I would step from my cell's confinement
calmly, cheerfully, firmly,
like a squire from his country-house.

Who am I? They often tell me
I would talk to my warders
freely and friendly and clearly,
as though it were mine to command.

Who am I? They also tell me
I would bear the days of misfortune
equably, smilingly, proudly,
like one accustomed to win.

Am I then really all that which other men tell of?
Or am I only what I know of myself,
restless and longing and sick, like a bird in a cage,
struggling for breath, as though hands were compressing
　　　　my throat,
yearning for colours, for flowers, for the voices of birds,
thirsting for words of kindness, for neighbourliness,
trembling with anger at despotisms and petty humiliation,
tossing in expectation of great events,
powerlessly trembling for friends at an infinite distance,
weary and empty at praying, at thinking, at making,
faint, and ready to say farewell to it all?
Who am I? This or the other?
Am I one person today, and tomorrow another?
Am I both at once? A hypocrite before others,

reflections

and before myself a contemptibly woebegone weakling?
Or is something within me still like a beaten army,
fleeing in disorder from victory already achieved?

Who am I? They mock me, these lonely questions of mine.
Whoever I am, thou knowest, O God, I am thine.[6]

Bonhoeffer struggled with the contradictions between his own self-perceptions and the ways others viewed him. The challenge of seeing ourselves rightly—seeing ourselves as God sees us—is an ongoing process of discovery. We are enabled to see ourselves more clearly when we commit ourselves to daily practices of scrutiny, opening ourselves up before God through confession and repentance as well as submitting ourselves to communities of people we know and trust well enough to hold us accountable in the faith.

The challenge of seeing ourselves rightly—seeing ourselves as God sees us—is an ongoing process of discovery.

Yet sometimes the challenge of healthy self-awareness is not so much failing to see but rather seeing in a way that produces fear and difficulty. Matthew's account of the Transfiguration uses the baptismal affirmation "This is my Son, the Beloved; with him I am well pleased" (17:5; see also 3:17). And then Matthew adds the phrase "Listen to him!" In other words, the voice of God is telling the disciples who are witnessing the Transfiguration, "Pay attention to what I'm doing through him." But the disciples are immediately overcome with fear. They are summoned by God to pay attention, but they find it over-

reflections

whelming. They fall on the ground, gripped by fear. When you read the story carefully, you see that it is not the Transfiguration itself that causes their fear, for Peter speaks to Jesus calmly after the Transfiguration. Their fear is connected to the voice from heaven speaking. And why are the disciples afraid? Their fearfulness might be connected to the phrase "Listen to him!" that Matthew adds.

This passage ends with Jesus predicting his own suffering and death (17:11-12). Could it be that in truly listening to him, in having "ears to hear and eyes to see," the disciples begin to glimpse the reality that this path—the path of suffering—is the one they must choose too?

Only when Jesus goes to his disciples and touches them are they able to rise and journey with him down the mountain. It takes the touch of Jesus to break their fear. As we learn to listen to him, we also discover that the journey will take us down paths we may fear; paths of self-discovery may cause us to see our shortcomings and self-deceptions. Or it may be that we discern the good in our lives we've been fearful to claim. What would it mean for Jesus to touch us today—to assure us that God searches us and knows our inward thoughts and still loves us completely? Our challenge is to let the touch of Jesus break our fearfulness and allow us to move in fresh and new ways down the path of discipleship. Let's listen to Jesus and follow him in living the good life.

reflections

FAITHFUL FRIENDS: WATCHING OVER ONE ANOTHER IN LOVE

Use this space to record thoughts, reflections, insights, prayer concerns, or other matters that arise from your weekly conversations with faithful friends.

—5—

Listening Alone, Listening Together

PSALM FOR PRAYING

Psalm 46:1-3, 10-11

God is our refuge and strength,
   a very present help in
      trouble.
Therefore we will not fear,
   though the earth should
   change,
though the mountains shake
   in the heart of the sea;
though its waters roar and
      foam,
   though the mountains
      tremble with its tumult.

"Be still, and know that I am
      God!
   I am exalted among the
      nations,
   I am exalted in the earth."
The LORD of hosts is with us;
   the God of Jacob is our
      refuge.

DAILY READINGS

DAY ONE
Mark 1:35; 6:46; Matthew 14:23 *(Jesus prays alone)*

DAY TWO
Luke 6:12-16 *(Jesus prays before the calling of the disciples)*

DAY THREE
Luke 11:1-4 *(Jesus and his disciples at prayer)*

DAY FOUR

John 17 *(Jesus prays for his disciples)*

DAY FIVE

Philippians 1:3-19; 4:1-7; Colossians 1:3-10 *(Intercessory prayer)*

DAY SIX

Read the chapter on pages 50–55. You may take notes in the space provided at the bottom of each page.

THE WESTMINSTER SHORTER CATECHISM says that the chief goal of human life is "to glorify God, and to enjoy him forever."[7] Our enjoyment of God begins with a deep prayer life cultivated through habits of personal, individual prayer as well as prayer shared with others in the community.

The focus of our prayers follows a three-fold pattern:

- upward toward the transcendent God
- inward for personal spiritual growth
- outward in concern and intercession for the community

These three directions in prayer also signify three primary yearnings of human beings:

- relationship with God, the Transcendent One
- achievement of a healthy sense of self and significance in our own lives
- development of meaningful relationships with others lived out in community

Our prayer life is insufficient unless it includes both listening to God alone as well as listening to God in relationship with others in community.

CHRISTIAN CHARACTER IN CONTEXT

The New Testament tells us that Jesus regularly went away by himself to pray. In the Sermon on the Mount, he taught his followers, "Whenever you pray, go into your room and shut the door"

reflections

(Matthew 6:6). It's important to commune with God one on one, from deep within the recesses of our own hearts. The psalmist is saying this when he writes in Psalm 46:10, "Be still, and know that I am God!" Yet when we look at this verse more closely, we discover it is set in a context of other verses written in first person plural. The following verse says, "The LORD of hosts is with us; / the God of Jacob is our refuge." The whole community is being called to stillness. We are to be attentive to the voice of God not only when we are alone but also when we are in the midst of the people. Jesus went away by himself to a lonely place to pray, but he also prayed with his disciples. Our personal prayer life is greatly enhanced when we share it with others.

One way to do this is by turning everything else off—a radical idea today with cell phones ringing, pagers buzzing, televisions blaring, and e-mails popping up—and opening a Bible with a few friends. Find a passage that is meaningful to you and then "pray" it, perhaps using a sacred form of reading Scripture called *lectio divina*. This practice of praying Scripture is a way of listening to God. As you hear these verses of Scripture read aloud over and over again, with significant periods of silence in between, you listen for particular words from the passage that God might be speaking directly to you. You listen for ways the passage speaks to your life right now. After you have heard the reading a number of times, you listen for an invitation from God—something God might be calling you to do or be in response to the Word. If you practice lectio divina in a group, you close by offering to God a prayer for the others who have prayed with you, that they might be able to respond to the invitation God has offered them.

Lectio divina lets us practice listening to the Word because the long periods of silence between the passages open up space for us

reflections

to listen for the voice of God. It also helps us practice intercessory prayer as we become aware of the needs of others and of how God might be at work in their lives.

This practice of praying with Scripture gives us the time, space, and silence we need to be able to listen to God and to help us discern God's Spirit from the various cultural spirits that compete for our affections. The practice is enhanced when we are able to do it regularly with wise friends who can help us hear the voice of God more clearly. At times these friends may also come to see us as their guides as well. For the purposes of this study, we'll call such friends and mentors *faithful friends*. They make a difference in our lives in at least three important ways:

- They challenge the sins we have come to love.
- They affirm the gifts we are afraid to claim.
- They help us dream the dreams we otherwise wouldn't have imagined.

In the first place, faithful friends help challenge the sins we've come to love. We might feel okay when people we respect and trust call us out on things we're doing that we already know are wrong, in part because our conscience has already been working on us. It is much harder, though, to have people call us on things we don't really believe are wrong. Perhaps we rationalize and say that what we're doing really isn't so bad, or maybe we think, *Well, nobody's going to get hurt, so why not?* Perhaps we are so self-deceived that we don't even realize the harm we might be causing.

Faithful friends help challenge the sins we've come to love.

reflections

NATHAN AND DAVID

Recall the story of Nathan and David in 2 Samuel 12. David is guilty of having an affair with the wife of another man and then orchestrating the man's killing to try to cover things up. When the prophet Nathan describes a similar situation to King David, David reacts quickly, saying that the man should be held accountable and punished. Nathan then bravely says to the king, "You are the man!" (12:7). We need such friends in our lives who risk holding a mirror up to our faces, even when we don't want them to. Often we don't like others to hold us accountable, but we know in the end that they must. And we know these people need us to do the same for them.

Faithful friends affirm the gifts we are afraid to claim. It's nice when people tell us we've done a good job, but it's no surprise if they're talking about something we know we're already good at doing. Faithful friends are people who know us well enough to cultivate in us gifts they can see but we can't. Sometimes we're afraid to try new things. Sometimes we play old tapes of voices from the past that have told us we can't achieve much. Other times we become complacent and content to continue doing what is familiar and safe. People who know us well can help us live into the new future that God is creating. They help give us the courage to move beyond our fears and limitations. They will say things to us like, "I see God working in your life in this way. Have you ever considered becoming a lay reader? Or ministering in the soup kitchen? Or attending seminary, perhaps to discern a call to ordained ministry? You seem to have a gift with children. Have you ever helped a child learn to read?"

reflections

We need people in our lives like that. The apostle Paul had a friend named Barnabas. Barnabas (whose name means "encourager") gave the kind of support and encouragement that helped Paul follow God's call. We need friends who will do that for us. And people need us to do that for them as well.

Faithful friends help us dream dreams we otherwise wouldn't have imagined. In Ephesians 3:20, the apostle writes, "By the power at work within us [God] is able to accomplish abundantly far more than all we can ask or imagine." Faithful friends help us not only to begin to believe this but also to live it. It would be sufficient to say that God can do more than all we could ask or imagine, but the apostle intensifies it three times over by adding the words *abundantly, far,* and *more.* He wants us to know how great God's power at work through us can be to bring about good in our lives and in the life of world. We need friends who can help us live into that kind of future—the life abundant that Jesus has promised to all who follow him.

Faithful friends teach us how to listen to God more carefully because they take the time to get to know us well. We come to trust them with our most intimate concerns and needs, and friendship with them gives us a glimpse into what friendship with God is like.

Friendship with God is the only perfect friendship.

Yet no matter how near and dear they are to us, friends will always fail us at some point, whether through misunderstandings, shortcomings, or their own inevitable death. But friendship with God is the only perfect friendship. Prayer links us with the only one who will never fail us. So when it seems as though the earth is shaking and we find ourselves in soul-searching distress, or when our lives

reflections

seem just a bit out of sorts with personal struggles and changes, prayer is particularly important. It roots and grounds us in God. Remember the importance of prayer, because prayer will hold you to the one who will never change, the one Hebrews 13:8 tells us is the same "yesterday and today and forever." It is important to develop practices and patterns of prayer—both personal and corporate—that guide and shape our lives through the normal day-to-day routines of life as well as through life's toughest times. And in so doing, we, as Christians, may come to live the good life.

reflections

FAITHFUL FRIENDS: WATCHING OVER ONE ANOTHER IN LOVE

Use this space to record thoughts, reflections, insights, prayer concerns, or other matters that arise from your weekly conversations with faithful friends.

—6—

Planning the Next Steps Together

PSALM FOR PRAYING

Psalm 86:11-12

Teach me your way, O LORD,
   that I may walk in your truth;
     give me an undivided heart to revere
      your name.
I give thanks to you, O Lord my God,
     with my whole heart,
     and I will glorify your name forever.

OR THE PAST FEW WEEKS you have experienced the "Come and See" portion of this study, exploring aspects of the Christian character trait of attentiveness. You have learned about and reflected upon "Listening to the Right Voices," "Keeping Time," "Self-Awareness," and "Listening Alone, Listening Together." You have experienced psalms for praying and lectio divina to engage Scripture in a prayerful way. You have communicated regularly as faithful friends with another person in the group. You have learned all this in the company of other Christians who also seek God's "good life."

In the space provided below, take some time now to write about particular learnings from the previous sessions that have been meaningful or significant to you.

The time has come to move from understanding attentiveness to developing practices of attentiveness. It is time to "Go and Do" attentiveness in your group.

At your next session, you and your group will plan together how to "try out" what you have learned about the Christian character trait of attentiveness. Then, for the weeks to follow, you will put your plan into action, both as individuals and as a group.

Your group planning session will be most effective if each member, in preparation for the session, takes a few minutes to brainstorm ways in which the group can begin to practice attentiveness over the next six weeks during the "Go and Do" portion of the study.

On the pages that follow, you will see several boxes, each of which contains an idea prompt. These idea prompts are designed to help you imagine ways in which you and your group could put into practice what you have learned about attentiveness. Allow your mind to explore every possible avenue for embodying this notion of attentiveness in your life as a Christian. Resist the tendency to edit your ideas; instead, record all of them in the spaces provided. Be ready to share them with the group when you meet.

As you consider and record your ideas, keep in mind that ideas are only a part of Christian character. Christianity comes alive only when, inspired by ideas, we move into the world, practicing and embodying our faith. That's when we truly become the body of Christ and begin—haltingly at first but then with confidence and faith—living the good life together.

Lectio divina Scripture passages

Behavioral changes to make

Ministry events to consider

Mission work to conceive and implement

Speakers to invite

Field trips, retreats, pilgrimages to take

Books to read, movies to see

Other ideas

Endnotes

1. Adapted by permission from *50 Ways to Pray: Practices From Many Traditions and Times,* by Teresa A. Blythe (Abingdon Press, 2006); pages 45–47.
2. From a lecture delivered by Matthew Schlimm at Duke University Divinity School.
3. From *Receiving the Day,* by Dorothy C. Bass (Jossey-Bass Publishers, 2000); page 64.
4. From *Christ on Trial: How the Gospel Unsettles Our Judgement,* by Rowan Williams (HarperCollins Publishers, 2000); page 56.
5. See *The Culture of Disbelief: How American Law and Politics Trivialize Religious Devotion,* by Stephen L. Carter (Anchor Books, 1994).
6. Reprinted with the permission of Scribner, an imprint of Simon & Schuster Adult Publishing Group, from *Letters and Papers From Prison,* revised, enlarged edition, by Dietrich Bonhoeffer, copyright © 1953, © 1967, © 1971 by SCM Press Ltd.
7. From http://www.reformed.org/documents/wsc/index.html.

ACKNOWLEDGMENTS

Living the Good Life Together: A Study of Christian Character in Community is the result of a very good idea. The idea was that the church needed help in teaching God's people to cultivate patterns or practices of holy living—in other words, to learn to live a good life as defined by Scripture and exemplified by Jesus. This idea became the subject of a very fruitful conversation, thanks especially to the participation of Timothy W. Whitaker, Resident Bishop of the Florida Annual Conference of The United Methodist Church; L. Gregory Jones, Dean and Professor of Theology at Duke University Divinity School; and Paul W. Chilcote, Professor of Historical Theology and Wesleyan Studies at Asbury Theological Seminary in Florida. Their commitment to the idea and their contributions to the development process provided the vision and the impetus for this unique resource.